AMERICAN HERSTORY

AMERICAN HERSTORY

poems by
celeste doaks

WINNER OF THE BACKBONE PRESS CHAPBOOK CONTEST

BULL·CITY PRESS
DURHAM, NC

AMERICAN HERSTORY

Second Edition. Printed in the United States of America.

Library of Congress Catalog Data

ISBN: 978-1-949344-70-7 (paperback) doaks, celeste
American Herstory: poems.

Cover Image: *Michelle LaVaughn Robinson Obama*
Portrait by Amy Sherald, Oil on linen, 2018
National Portrait Gallery, Smithsonian Institution

Book Design: Crystal Simone Smith with Spock and Associates

....

Originally published in 2019 by Backbone Press, with support from the Durham Arts Council.

BULL CITY PRESS
1217 Odyssey Drive
Durham, NC 27713
www.BullCityPress.com

TABLE OF CONTENTS

for Preston and Perse
always

and of course

Michelle LaVaughn Obama

RESPONSE TO THE WHITE WOMAN IN NORTH CAROLINA WHO ASKS, "WHY ARE YOU WRITING MICHELLE OBAMA POEMS?"

Because she is the 1st lady of the United States of America
Because she is an orchid in the middle of America's desert
Because there are Jackie Onassis, Eleanor Roosevelt, Betty Ford
and Dolly Madison poems.
Because once I was a little girl who adored Molly Ringwald, Linda Carter
and Strawberry Shortcake.
Because black is definitely on my palette, even if it isn't on yours
Because Barack chose her
Because she chose Barack, and maybe the planets aligned (or Nostradamus
predicted it)
or maybe America finally just moved into its adulthood. Isn't it time
we move out, sign our names to a lease and start cooking our own
terrible casseroles?
Because America is a rainbow and not a monolith
Because your being uncomfortable makes me comfortable.
Because after Michelle there can be Marisol
Agnieszka
Suen Lee
Judd
or whatever the hell else we want it to be…

IN THE GARDEN WITH MICHELLE

~an imagined conversation

Long after the secret service have drifted into REM sleep, We start slow, our
voices carrying over the radishes, cabbages

and carrots. Covering everything from finding cheap drug store foundation
that matches our skin type, to how Donna Karan and Calvin

Klein don't build jeans for black thighs, and ways to moisturize brown skin
in summer. You advise against Vaseline, my family's

favorite, and sing the praiases of Nivea. We weigh in on hair products, perms
vs. naturals, braids, weaves, and extensions. Is Ultra Sheen

too greasy? Do flat irons create follicle damage? You add a few tidbits about
Barack, careful not to spill too many beans, as the hand-held augur

digs deeper. Black dirt and worms come up, as you admit overhearing some
white house chefs whispering about having to cook for a black woman.

The silent flip-flops your stomach turned.
You mention the burst of pride you felt replacing

the pastorals and still-lifes with abstracts in yellows
and blues. We rave about vegetarian dishes and our joint love

of sweets. I nod and confess my love of plain old vanilla ice cream.
You lean in, smiling and ask if I want to go inside and try one

of your Dark Chocolate chip cookies.

"FLOTUS WINS FIRST LADY COOKIE CONTEST" OR THE OATS MIGHT WIN RONDEAU

"One cannot think well, love well, sleep well, if one has not dined well." ~Virginia Woolf

The oats might win, but taste like crap
The crowd may cheer and shout and clap
Beneath their smiles complete disgrace
Revealing color's their true race
Not cookies, egos rule the map

No praline filled with loads of sap
Or other kind, will slim the gap
The lovely ladies always face
The oats might win!

And Mrs. O might see the trap
The biased rules, the leaking tap
Bouquet of daisies, in cracked vase
Please throw them into outer space!
Your White and Dark bites are the hap,
(Who cares) the Oats might win!!

IN THE GARDEN WITH MICHELLE, PART II

~an imagined conversation

We decide to have our sweets on the green, out among
the few dandelions, basil wafting past our noses.

She speaks of times when Barack didn't bring roses, rough
Senatorial races, and woes about where to school the girls.

Not that men are secondary, but with rates of HIV rising
like hot air balloons among straight black women,

we are both more than concerned. I confess I couldn't believe
Cindy won the first bake off. "There's always more than food

at stake," you say. Approval ratings, voter confidence. Making
a blue crack in a red sky. Things most of America wants. We

move on to motherhood and you reminisce about all the pants
your mother let out, the hems undone like unfulfilled wishes.

And right before we part, you harvest some chard, placing it
in your basket. You add it may be on tomorrow's menu.

I balk about how bikini bottoms never fit black behinds
properly and you chuckle saying "fit is only a state of mind."

INVESTIGATING THE BLACK FEMALE LARGE POSTERIOR OR HOT BOOTY

~a response to republican Senator Sensenbrenner who was overheard saying that Michelle Obama should practice what she preaches. He said she lectures on healthy eating but has a "large posterior" herself.

Can you please describe a hot booty? Does it wrinkle up and fester in the sun or does it grow to the size of a large ego, until ripe for picking?

Hot bootys sparkle like the rainbow, shoot gold-covered shit and obliterate all possibilities of sitting naked on a beanbag. Hot bootys smile as if hiding an ancient Chinese secret, but usually are of African descent. If questioned, hot bootys generally remain silent knowing anything they murmur can and will be used against them. But silence is difficult considering they give themselves away by smelling like frankincense and myrrh. Honestly, hot bootys are so hot they might spontaneously combust if left alone for excess amounts of time.

What are some habits of hot bootys? Are they nocturnal or diurnal? Do they congregate often or travel in packs?

Almost all hot bootys love fried foods. You can find them strung out at KFC, Mickey D's or Popeye's. Even if they're at a Chinese joint they'll order a side of French fries. Pathetic. Hot bootys are recently migrating south. Like the yellow warbler, his chirp a sweet song reeling you in, they are finding warmer climates welcoming. And while they do travel in packs, herds, or flocks they are more valuable when collected individually. Think
J-Lo. Think Kim Kardashian. Think Michelle Obama.

If we take a picture of one, will you be able to identify it?

If included in a police lineup, hot bootys will stand out. They are always to blame and forever the culprit. If you're not careful they'll even hypnotize you. The sneaky little mothers. And in the end, will plead for forgiveness but know the judge's gavel gets heavy at the mere sight of a hot booty. They can be spotted a mile away with their bulbous exterior. And the easiest way to catch them is to pull them over on the highway, their collage of red, yellows, and purples trailing behind them, bathed in iridescence.

BLACK BARBIE

~for psychologists and married couple Kenneth and Mamie Clark, who completed a study on dolls in the 1940's which showed that children, despite their color, prefer white dolls over brown dolls.

Luckily, I can recall when
you were released
Long silky hair
Full brown bosom

Momma brought you home, elated
to possess one
Mattel's phenom
Her prize dujour

Inauguration day presents
A living one
Draped in white, our
First Lady doll

WHAT THE FIRST LADY FOUND IN MY HOMAGE

~inspired by the abstract painting by Joseph Albers entitled "Homage to the Square: Elected II."

At first the connections wouldn't come to my eyes. I only saw
separate stars hanging amid a black night. My work a Big Dipper
not yet discovered; but she found softness in my squares, complexity
in my simplicity. A steely grey hugging a cerulean blue; that blue

spooning the marigold center, holding on tight to love. In my painting
she found something holy, something worth traveling to, like
the Ganges River, the water a blue blessing. Perhaps she found
my chromatic interactions a bit poetic, each hue defining the other,

a metaphor hard to decipher, but easy to feel. And my four corners
probably reveal more about my Germanic upbringing than I care to admit. But
she found vulnerability of this outsider looking for home, a recognition of
herself or maybe her husband in it. She understood my abstractions

rooted in discipline, like an architect rising to his drawing board
each morning at five, reworking last night's sketches. Eyes
blood shot dark. Despite the hard edges, in my homage she
found all the bridges bringing the sky just a bit closer to earth.

BLACK LOTUS VILLANELLE

Lotus rising out of South Side water & night
Gifting the world with your brilliant fruitful flower
We marvel at your beauty; bless your seeds with light

You bloom ivy, league that is, grow tall in their sight
Defying every shallow pond with fierce power
Lotus rising out of South Side water & night

Your floral family hails from a deep southern plight
Ancestors fertilize the A.M.E. church hour
We marvel at your beauty; bless your seeds with light

For three days your petals bloom gallant as a knight
Picture that - Monet paints you in sun or shower
Lotus rising out of South Side water & night

How many six-foot stalks revel in their rare height?
Dark pods don't flinch; stand stoic as a light tower
We marvel at your beauty; bless your seeds with light

Stem of Third World Center, Egyptians know your rite
We pray you never wane or retreat to bower
Lotus rising out of South Side water & night
We marvel at your beauty; bless your seeds with light

MALIA & SASHA SPEAK, A CONTRAPUNTAL

We both
Are sisters
Were birthed
In the fever
Of our parents' love.
Almost mirror each other
I try to lead, but
Sometimes fall short
So, I'll just jam to Beyoncé
Knowing we are dad's halos
Not always shined to perfection

attend Sidwell Friends
where prim girls grow
my sister and I
obsessed with tennis and piano
Still, our corn-silked black strands
reflect grace and style.
Animal dander and 'privileged' comments
make Malia mad
tapping her feet
getting closer to all grown up
but hurdling over life's building blocks

FOR "SKY LIGHT"

~inspired by an Alma Thomas painting also acquired by the Obamas

1

Say you the blue magic   cosmic shit
that got to stay   Say   you were the underdog
the amateur   with no wins or sparkly belt to boast
who was never expected to take the title in the third round
everything about you   risky and inviting   Say
you the aurora borealis   born from the charged particles
of a woman named Thomas   The whole of you a collision
between polar opposites   Say spectacular   Say sacred
Say shimmer   like it's your only show

2

"Watusi" envies me, but I'm green
for her chic name which invokes
a Chubby Checker dance.
Her bold patches, collage-like,
sing across the page.
Each one another elegant note.
Everyone compares her to a Matisse.
That can't be bad. Imitation is the
sincerest form and should be the
battery charging your machine.
Instead, you sulk but we are both
born of her womb,
and have done pretty well for ourselves.
You bow your head, drag your
feet, but just think multiple others
were passed over.
How many others would give anything to be
linked to American Herstory?
How wonderful to be
her daily inspiration (or his) like a
prayer book bringing comfort on
sleepless nights.

3

My Catalina blues captured her, the singular columns,
line up behind a blank slate of white. I explode, determined
as a black school child segregated from white children,
white schools. My color bleeds through cracks, infectious.
How can you not love me? Born in '73, the second child,
the family's baby in every way, struggling for your attention.
I am the tapestry of America, color infused with light,
come to tell my story.

MRS. O PICKS "INTERTWINING SCROLLS" FOR THE OVAL OFFICE

~in the voice of Jeri Redcorn, artist and member of the Native American Caddo tribe

I etched that pot with bone and sharp metal tools;
the surfaces scraping together like cricket legs
making their nocturnal music. I rubbed red clay
into each design, obsessed with perfection.
After sixty-five days my hands knew its surface,
the same way I know each mole on my husband's back.
My fingers blistered and peeling, nothing could console.
I almost gave up; the overdue bills creeping in, haunting
my days and nights. But despite life's attempts to snuff out
this creative desire, the land's heartbeat is smarter than us;
an October harvest moon called me back to the wood fire,
the hand coiled, the Caddo Way. So when the phone rung,
part of me shrank into myself. The thought of ravens danced
in my brain, but a red cardinal won out. His chirp sent my pot
into her hands, into that office, close to the President's left.
I know when he gazes at it, conversation will happen.
And even though my ancestors are long gone, I bet they
will still hear the exchange, the melody of praise in the distance.

THE LINKED HISTORIES THAT PLAGUE US

~for Michelle Obama's father, Fraser C. Robinson, and my Aunt Vie

Did it start with a tingling, that strange almost ticklish
sensation plaguing the fingertips?

My aunt met death in her Chevrolet,
Smoky Robinson defiantly blasting, a blood vessel
in her brain ballooning to an abnormal width—

Or perhaps the saliva wouldn't go down, no matter how
many times he swallowed. His will not enough to damn
the body to orders.

Eventually the base of her brain flooded, leaving
a long blue silence after the tape deck went to fuzz.

In those strange twilight moments, could he smell the faint scent
of muscles rebelling? Did he know they were already growing
tired of the fight?

What is hereditary, what is our fate? In those times
when you were lifting Sasha into a swing, or reaching
for a can of Campbell's in the kitchen cabinet, and you felt
a dull numbing in your right arm, did you panic for a few seconds,
as I do, a family member slowly coming into consciousness,
like an unavoidable déjà vu snippet?

JUMPING FIT HAIKU

~inspired by Mrs. Obama's *Let's Move!* Initiative

children jump rope as
lungs expand with gratitude
under summer sun

FOR "WATUSI (HARD EDGE)"

~an abstract painting by Alma Thomas picked for Mrs. O's East Wing office, then was removed soon after because it did not "fit the space."

Draped in disparate blues Maya, Tiffany, Azure, Cobalt, all play
against each other; their melodies Miles, harmonies Thelonious

A few greens, a mint or sea, sandwiched under a wicked marigold,
the yellow of the daffodils Mariah tried to convince Lucy to adore, the hue
so alluring

In the right-hand corner, a baby pink barely brushing a grey like a
familiar lover, or raindrops falling over brownstones in Brooklyn

A red, its backbone pressed against the right-hand wall, a tall drink
of water, bold, unwavering, reverberating off its partner orange
across the way   But the stand out is the lone black panel,

surrounded by white spaces, deeper than the earth's mantle,
an inner core hard as steel wool, and complex as an aria
The letters on a book not yet written, the pepper in the pot of soup,
a quarter note on a five-bar staff, a whisper turned into a shout

RIGHT TO BARE HER ARMS HAIKU

~inspired by Mrs. O's sleeveless dresses, exposed bare arms and #sleevegate

In spring it's her right
to proudly bear them. Then quote
second amendment.

MICHELLE OBAMA'S PINTEREST INTEREST SONNET

~inspired by her dissertation written on the discrimination and isolation she faced at Princeton, opening a Pinterest page, and appeal to the digital age

She knows a picture's worth a million
blurbs, not Polaroid or disposable,
but on Internet, it's controllable.
Securing her fans, pleasing civilians.

So far, on her own she has posted eight,
with White House staff posting the other four,
but will her contributions ever bore??
Somehow, I doubt it; masses love the bait!

So far she's pinned her and the Pres kissing,
Another of her winning tug-of-war,
a garden shot, hands in dirt, nothing more.
Our prim first lady, with nothing missing.

But will we ever see Princeton's distaste
The jeers, and high ivory mountains you faced?

KISSING THE WHITE HOUSE WALLS

~written in the voice of Glenn Ligon's avant-garde visual art installation entitled "Black Like Me II"

(Emotion) Meaning blurred like my letters, she picked me,
my back-story difficult (easy) as apple pie. Crust tanning from white
to brown like a (50-year-old beach bum) first edition copy of Black
Beauty. Both dying to be in your hands. How I (we) got here, I'm unsure.
Standing amid a Rothko, and bronze Degas sculptures, I am an arrogant
teenager full of truths (lies) that sting my lips. Their sounds
reverberating off ivory mantles and mahogany desks. This is the life
(millisecond) I always dreamed of. To exist here with them, my corners
kissing these White House walls.

AMERICAN HERSTORY

Tell them it's always under attack. Tell them there's no cure
for the disease, or answer to the riddle. Tell them you asked many
before you, some who won, some who lost.

You consulted Assata, Roe vs. Wade, Harriet and Joycelyn Elders
to no avail. Her words on contraception twisted into a bitter pretzel.
The bits broken off, used to destroy her.

Tell them it's always under attack, its predators everywhere. They lurk
behind Mississippi clinics or around Georgetown blocks dressed
in blue uniform. Tell them you have the cure, somewhere at home,

deep in your cabinets, mixed in a mason jar, don't tell them
it consists of breast milk, dreams, butterflies, civil rights marches,
burned bras, a piece of Madame CJ Walker's hair, prayers,
Amelia Earhart's drive, hot-water cornbread, and Sally Ride's fearlessness.

Lie to them, tell them it's rosemary oil, then bottle it. Sell it
to every woman in America who will drink it. Then watch all
the naysayers disappear.

ACKNOWLEDGMENTS

Obsidian Magazine Literature in the African Diaspora: "Black Barbie"

Obsidian Magazine Literature in the African Diaspora: "Black Lotus"

Split This Rock Poem of the Week: "American Herstory"

Squaw Valley Review: "In the Garden with Michelle II"

Beltway Poetry Quarterly: "For Watusi (Hard Edge)"

***

In addition to the journals and online publications mentioned above, I'd like to extend my thanks to all of the organizations who've supported me while these poems were incubating. Sending love to the Split This Rock Organization, Community of Writers at Squaw Valley, Carolina African American Writers Collective, Ivy Bookshop, Enoch Pratt Library, CityLit Project, Eubie Blake Cultural Center, Rubys Artist Grants and the Robert W. Deutsch foundation.

I'd like to acknowledge teachers and friends who provide me with such joie de vivre. While this collection came together over a few years, there are some folks who always deserve special thanks for a variety of reasons. Whether you traveled 3 hours to hear me read or just lent me your ear to vent, I stan you. Dorianne Laux, Patricia Smith, Sharon Olds, Sarah Browning, Niki Herd, Russ Litten. My NC State fam: William Badger, Wilton Barnhardt, Shailen Mishra, Sheila Smith McKoy and Jake Young. My University of Delaware fam: Stephanie Kerschbaum, McKay Jenkins, and Tiffany Barber.

To my Baltimore/DMV literary family: Michael Tager and Ian Anderson of Mason Jar Press, Tafisha Edwards, Teri Cross Davis, Black Ladies Brunch Collective, Steven Leyva, Anthony Moll, Mary Sherman Willis, Joseph Ross, Ailish Hopper, Jane Satterfield, Judy Cooper, Tracy Dimond, Emma Snyder, Carla Dupree, Ed Berlin.

And my personal road dogs Lydia Rhodes, Chyno (AKA The Boy with the Blue Beard), Katie Worth, Carol Bruce & Mike, Wendy and Douglas, and Julie and Brad.

Lastly, I'm always indebted to my chosen family: Mom, Dad, Ced, CJ, Cameron and Karl. Your love and support keep me afloat during any storm.

ABOUT THE AUTHOR

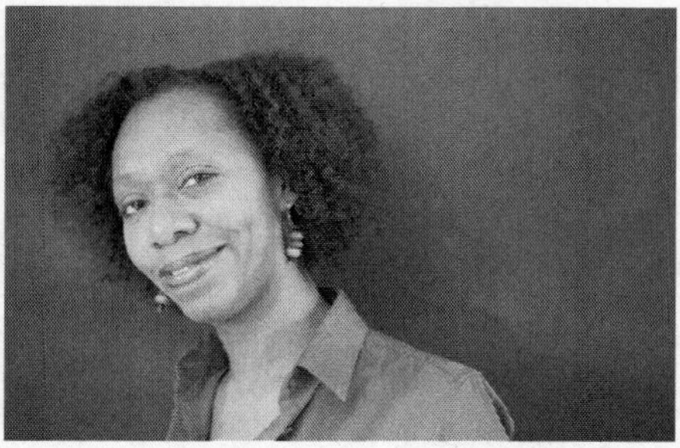

celeste doaks is the author of *Cornrows and Cornfields* (2015) and editor of the poetry anthology *Not Without Our Laughter* (2017). Since the initial publication of *American Herstory* in 2019, poems from the collection have been featured at the Whitney Museum of American Art, the Smithsonian American Art Museum, and Brooklyn Museum. She's been a university professor for over a decade, and is also a 2022 Yaddo fellow. Her work has appeared in multiple US and UK online and print publications including *Ms.*, *The Millions, Huffington Post, Chicago Quarterly Review, The Hopkins Review,* and many others. Currently, she lives in Baltimore with her husband and too many house plants; and she teaches poetry in the Fairfield University and Hood College low-residency programs.

ABOUT THE COVER ART

Michelle LaVaughn Robinson Obama
By Amy Sherald
Oil on linen
2018

National Portrait Gallery, Smithsonian Institution

Gift of Kate Capshaw and Steven Spielberg; Judith Kern and Kent Whealy; Tommie L. Pegues and Donald A. Capoccia; Clarence, DeLoise, and Brenda Gaines; Jonathan and Nancy Lee Kemper; The Stoneridge Fund of Amy and Marc Meadows; Robert E. Meyerhoff and Rheda Becker; Catherine and Michael Podell; Mark and Cindy Aron; Lyndon J. Barrois and Janine Sherman Barrois; The Honorable John and Louise Bryson; Paul and Rose Carter; Bob and Jane Clark; Lisa R. Davis; Shirley Ross Davis and Family; Alan and Lois Fern; Conrad and Constance Hipkins; Sharon and John Hoffman; Audrey M. Irmas; John Legend and Chrissy Teigen; Eileen Harris Norton; Helen Hilton Raiser; Philip and Elizabeth Ryan; Roselyne Chroman Swig; Josef Vascovitz and Lisa Goodman; Eileen Baird; Dennis and Joyce Black Family Charitable Foundation; Shelley Brazier; Aryn Drake-Lee; Andy and Teri Goodman; Randi Charno Levine and Jeffrey E. Levine; Fred M. Levin and Nancy Livingston, The Shenson Foundation; Monique Meloche Gallery, Chicago; Arthur Lewis and Hau Nguyen; Sara and John Schram; Alyssa Taubman and Robert Rothman

A NOTE ABOUT THE TEXT

The typeface used in the titles and text are:
Avenir designed by Adrian Frutiger, 1988 &
Palatino designed by Hermann Zapf, 1949

This book was originally published by Backbone Press, printed and bound in the United States of America. It was reissued by Bull City Press.